HOW TO DEAL WITH
Verbal Aggression

HOW TO DEAL WITH
Verbal Aggression

Robert Agar-Hutton FFA MIAP MICM

Matador
12 Manor Walk, Coventry Road, Market Harborough, Leics LE16 9BP, UK
Tel: (+44) 1858 468828 / 469898   Email: books@troubador.co.uk   Web: www.troubador.co.uk/matador

ISBN 1 899293 78 7

The publishers and author have made every effort to ensure the accuracy of information presented in this book; however, they can accept no responsibility for any loss, injury or inconvenience sustained by any person as a result of advice contained in the book.

Typesetting: Troubador Publishing Ltd, Market Harborough, UK
Printed and bound by Cambrian, Wales

Matador is an imprint of Troubador Publishing Ltd

CONTENTS

v

ACKNOWLEDGEMENTS

Firstly thanks to my wife Lee and my children Ben, Jason and Mel, all of whom helped me tidy up this book into a readable format. More importantly thanks to them for their support and love.

Thanks to my proof-reader Penny Williams for translating some of my sometimes idiosyncratic English into a more understandable form.

Thanks to my publisher Jeremy Thompson for his help in all the matters of production and in answering the endless stream of completely naive questions that I asked.

A huge "Thank you" to all the teachers, tutors, mentors and other people who have helped me develop my ability to understand and deal with aggression. Equally "Thank you" to all the people who have attended the training courses that I have given, I have learnt so much from you all.

Finally, thank you for choosing to read this book. I hope that in here, you will find the advice and information that you need.

ABOUT THE AUTHOR

Robert Agar-Hutton was born in London, England in 1953. He left school at age 17 to enter the accountancy profession and at the same age he started what has ever since been a major interest in the history and practice of the martial and health arts. Ten years later he gave up his accountancy practice and moved into selling, supporting and writing software for personal computers. In 1987 he started Protectics to teach courses in aggression, violence and stress management.

His accomplishments and interests are extremely varied ranging from science fiction to hard science, practical first aid to Reiki, Photography to Internet marketing strategies. He is a fellow of the Association of Financial Accountants, a member of the Institute of Programmers and Analysts, and a member of the Institute of Conflict Management. He is a third degree black belt in Karate and a Tai Chi instructor. Robert also gives after-dinner speeches and lectures on the subjects of aggression and stress management.

Most importantly (to him) he has been happily married since 1981 and has three children who fill his life with interest, excitement and a regular opportunity to practice his stress and aggression management skills.

OVERVIEW

This book will help you deal with people who are angry and are being verbally aggressive towards you. You will learn:

◆   How to recognise the causes of anger.

◆   Techniques that will enable you to defend yourself from harm.

◆   How to achieve win-win solutions, where both you and the person who is being aggressive will be able to finish in a calm state where resolution of differences is possible.

The book is aimed primarily at people who face aggression within the context of work. However, the techniques are also valid in a personal context when dealing with strangers, friends or family.

Style

This book is designed as an interactive workbook. You can simply read it and gain a lot of information. However, if you work through all the questionnaires and tests you will, through participation, learn and make the techniques your own. The benefit will be greatly enhanced.

Apology

I shall start this book with an apology. It contains some bad language. The reason is simple — this book will teach you how to deal with verbal aggression and a significant amount of verbal aggression contains bad language. So there is no point in trying to sidestep the issue or pretend it doesn't exist. If you want to be able to deal effectively and easily with people who swear, you have to get used to the terminology.

What is verbal aggression?

First a definition: "Verbal aggression is anger expressed vocally." This book does not deal with verbal bullying, which is often done with pretend anger in order to control an outcome in a pre-planned way. Verbal aggression is much more honest and generally more spontaneous.

I encourage you to devise your own definitions as you read this book. Indeed, if any of the information or techniques in this book are to be of real use to you, it is essential that you make them your own.

Terms

You will find that words such as annoyed, anger, and aggression are used almost interchangeably throughout this book. He and she are definitely interchangeable — women and men can and do become equally verbally aggressive.

Repetition

You may read something and think to yourself, "He's already said that". If you do, you will probably be right. Several points that I want to make are important enough to repeat. If you are blessed with total recall, I apologise. However if, like me, learning can be difficult sometimes, then you will benefit from the inbuilt revision.

Language

In this book, I have used 'English English'. So if you are an American reader you will find words like 'Ladybird' instead of 'Ladybug' and 'Postal Code' instead of 'Zip Code'. Also in the examples that mention money I have used the English '£' pound sign. If you find any other terms that do not 'translate' (or indeed any errors) please let me know and I'll put details of them in future editions of this book and on my website (at http://www.verbal-aggression.com) which is also where you can report any issues relating to the book. Of course if you speak any other flavour of English that also has differences, let me know and I'll make sure that the discrepancies are noted.

Disclaimer

I note (with growing apprehension) the tendency for people to blame others for their troubles and an increase in the amount of frivolous litigation. So unfortunately I need to say that whilst all the techniques mentioned in this book are effective, it is impossible to guarantee their safety or suitability for use in any specific scenario and it is for you, the reader, to determine how best to actually deal with somebody who is being aggressive towards you.

WHAT MAKES SOMEONE ANGRY?

Have you ever been angry? I suspect the answer is yes. I once met a woman who said that she had never been angry, but I confess that I didn't believe her. From time to time things happen that make us feel annoyed, frustrated and angry. It's human nature.

Think about the things that make you angry.

Write some of them down.

You can write in this book, or if you prefer, use a sheet of paper.

THINGS THAT MAKE ME ANGRY:

1.

2.

3.

4.

5.

6.

Now let's examine what causes anger.

Look back at the things that make you angry and you will find that they almost certainly fall into one of the following three categories.

1   Being scared

If something scares you there are a range of feelings and actions that may occur. One response to being scared is to become angry.

There is a well documented human response called the 'Fight or Flight' response. When we are scared our body prepares itself for either 'fight' or 'flight'. Part of the 'Fight' response is to become aggressive and angry. For most people, it's easy to see how this happens when dealing with another person. However sometimes it is difficult to understand why things can scare you and make you angry.

Imagine that you are opening your post. There is a bill addressed to you for £500 from a company you have never heard of. They appear to want money from you. You might phone them and be just a little bit angry. Why? Because the unexpected demand for money has frightened you.

You are waiting in traffic. You start to worry that you will be late for work or late home. You imagine your boss or wife being displeased. You get worried (a little bit frightened) then you become angry.

Look back at your original list and see if any of the things that make you angry fit this category. If they don't, then use the space on the next page to list a couple of things that might make you scared and then angry.

1. ....

2. ....

2 Being hurt

People often get angry when they are hurt. Perhaps whilst you are in the supermarket, someone knocks into you with a trolley or at work a co-worker spills hot coffee on you.

Imagine that when you phone up to complain about the bill for £500 from the company you have never heard of, it turns out that the name of the company is different from the name of a store where you did order goods. You'd forgotten about it and you do indeed have to pay out £500.

Physically, emotionally, financially or otherwise — being hurt can cause anger.

Look back at your original list and see if any of the things that make you angry fit this category. If they don't, then use the space below to list a couple of things that might hurt you and then make you angry.

1. ....

2. ....

3　　　　　　　　　　　　　　　　　　**Being ignored**

This makes me (and many other people) really angry. You may be waiting in a queue while some seemingly incompetent person tries to deal with the obviously easy problem of the person in front. Or you may be talking to someone and their attention keeps wandering. They are not listening to you but idly gazing around the room. Being ignored can often be the 'final straw' that drives somebody who is upset or worried into loud and aggressive behaviour.

Look back at your original list and see if any of the things that make you angry fit this category. If they don't, then use the space below to list some ways you could be ignored that might make you angry.

1.　_____

2.　_____

Other things that cause anger

There may well be other things that make you angry. I've talked to several hundred people and I've always found that one of the above three reasons is the root cause.

If other things make you angry, that's fine. Be aware of all the reasons why people become annoyed and learn to watch out for them. Then you won't become angry yourself, and you won't do things that make others angry.

A little game

Over the next two or three weeks, whenever you become angry or see someone else becoming angry, try to see the underlying reason and keep a scorecard. At the end of a week it might look like this:

	Me	Others
Scared	3	7
Hurt	2	12
Ignored	3	9

It should help you realise two important things:

◆ What makes you most angry.

◆ That other people are different from you and may have different triggers for their anger.

Photocopy the form on page 10 and keep it with you to record your findings.

WHAT CAUSES ANGER?

	Me	Others
Being scared		
Being hurt		
Being ignored		

WHAT TYPES OF ANGER?

What are the main ways in which anger is displayed? Do they have any effect on how you should deal with that aggression? Let's start by defining them. It's good to have labels for different behaviours, as it will help us choose the optimal responses for dealing with them.

List below the different ways in which you think people might display anger.

1. _____

2. _____

3. _____

4. _____

People exhibit anger in four main ways...

1   Being sullen and withdrawn

If someone is sullen and withdrawn they may not want to discuss anything. Since this book is about dealing with verbal aggression and not how to counsel people with problems, we'll leave them be (for now).

2   Being obstructive

It's not nice when someone is obstructive and you need to think about how to deal with this type of behaviour, but once again it's outside the scope of this book.

3   Verbal, maybe abusive

Now we're getting to the good stuff. When they become angry many people express it verbally. They may be loud, quiet, pleading, threatening or rude — sometimes extremely rude.

4   Physical violence

Most people when angry will express it verbally, then, if the verbal stage is not dealt with, they may become violent. However, you should remember and be aware that some people miss out the verbal stage, going straight from anger to action. If you are the focus of that anger, it can be dangerous.

You must decide whether these definitions are too few, too many, or just right. Everybody encodes their experiences slightly differently, based on beliefs, past experiences, rules that they have learned and a thousand and one other factors. You need enough pigeon holes in which to classify the different behaviours, but not so many that you confuse yourself.

REVISION TEST ONE .

List the three basic causes of anger.

1. _____

2. _____

3. _____

List the four basic ways people display anger.

1. _____

2. _____

3. _____

4. _____

Remember the last time you felt angry, and write down the cause.

_____

_____

Remember the last time you saw someone else become angry, and write down the way they displayed it.

_____

_____

RULES OF ENGAGEMENT

To deal with any situation, such as making an omelette, fixing a broken watch, or dealing with aggressive behaviour, we need procedures and rules. It will help you if the rules that you use (I refer to them as 'Rules of engagement') are generally applicable rather than specific.

There are four rules that you should always try to remember.

1 Have fun

Everything that you do has a positive and a negative side: you can be an optimist or a pessimist, the choice is yours. (Think about that for a moment — you alone are in control of your thoughts and feelings). So whenever you do anything, look for the fun, the enjoyment and the positive side.

Someone is unhappy and is screaming and shouting at you. Where is the fun? How about the enjoyment you get out of seeking a solution that will make the person stop being unhappy. If that's too difficult, then how about the enjoyment you will get by seeking a solution that will make them stop screaming and shouting at you.

List here three things that you think are fun.

1. _____

2. _____

3. _____

2   You can control your universe

The things that happen to you, only happen to 'you' once you are aware of them. 'You' is a term that almost implicitly implies consciousness. Thus it is up to you how you view the world.

You can even go further.

You can take responsibility.

Assume that you and you alone are the source of all the positive and negative things that happen. What does this let you do? It lets you take credit for all the good things "Yippee, I'm wonderful, look how beautiful the weather is today." When negative things happen it empowers you, because you know that you can make things positive.

"But what if I can't" is a question I'm often asked. The answer is simple: would you rather consider yourself to be a sailing ship at the mercy of the storm blown this way and that, or a ship with a powerful engine that tries to control its route and reach a safe harbour?

"That's not the way the real world is" is another response that I sometimes get. This implies that the rules that govern existence (and our interaction with things) are known. This is simply not true. Nobody knows how the universe works; we (including the greatest scientists, philosophers and religious leaders) are all making guesses. Some of those guesses may be inspired by outside agents, some may withstand the rigours of scientific methodology, and some may simply feel right or make sense. However, it is not possible to prove them at this time.

I suggest therefore that it is worthwhile making a guess that empowers us rather than one that diminishes us. Believe that you can rather than you can't and you may well succeed. Believe that you can't rather than you can and, not surprisingly, you won't succeed.

Our beliefs, our attitudes and our actions are important and can make a difference.

EXERCISE

Think of all the things (large and small) that you control and list them here.

3   Be determined to be agreeable

This one is fun and puts you in control. In every situation, try to be agreeable. Don't be a doormat, allowing people to walk all over you. Don't be a bombastic, arrogant 'Son of a bitch' who is rude to everyone. Decide that you will be polite yet forceful, courteous and resourceful.

If you get into a conflict situation with this determination, then you have already started to formulate a solution. If you go in with any other mindset (even a neutral one), you may find that you are adding to the problem.

Try the following affirmations (either out loud or in the privacy of your mind).

I will like everyone I meet and they will like me.

I can solve any problem that I encounter.

I am always pleasant and have time and a friendly word for everyone.

In conflict I will be relaxed and resourceful.

4   Every problem is resolvable

In the real world some problems have no solution, so what can you do? The simple and elegant answer is to say "Sod the real world." and proceed on the basis that every problem is resolvable. Think about it. If you start working on a problem when you know it's difficult or impossible, what are your chances of success? Slim at best. If, however, you face the problem with optimism and a can-do attitude, there is a chance (and often a very good chance) that you will resolve that problem. You may even invent a new solution. Remember that everything was new once, be it physics, mathematics, art, engineering, or language. Everything has been created by someone who faced a problem and decided that they had to find a solution.

Buy yourself a small pocket diary or notebook and keep a log of all your triumphs. Whenever you face a problem (no matter how small) and deal with it successfully, write it in the book. If there is a problem that you cannot resolve, just ignore it. After a while you will have a booklet full of your successes. When you review them (even after a few months) you will be delighted to find that you are a successful and resourceful person. Indeed, you will probably find that the act of noting down your successes will increase the number of successes you have. It creates an evidence trail and a positive feedback loop.

THE SCIENCE OF CYBERNETICS

What is cybernetics?

It is a term coined in 1948 by Norbert Wiener, an American mathematician. It refers to the general analysis of control and communication systems in living organisms and machines.

It is derived from the Greek word *kybernetes* ("steersman" or "governor").

What, you may be wondering, has cybernetics got to do with dealing with verbal aggression? The answer is a heck of a lot.

Let's look at one of the fundamental laws of cybernetics.

It's called the Law of Requisite Variety, and it has been defined in a variety of ways:

1) "In any system of human beings or machines, the element in that system with the widest range of variability will be the controlling element."

2) "The greater the variety within a system, the greater its ability to reduce variety in its environment through regulation."

3) "The larger the variety of actions available to a

21

control system, the larger the variety of perturbations it is able to compensate."

4)　"The element in a system that has the most flexibility will be the controlling, or catalytic, element in that system."

What this means to us is:

The more you know
and the more you can do,
the better are your chances
of succeeding

To put it another way, in any conflict situation, the greater the variety of responses that you have practised, the better are your chances for success.

You are adaptable

One of the nice things about being human is that we are extremely adaptable. We can learn new skills and we can discard old skills that are no longer working for us.

Think of the things you know now that you didn't know ten years ago, five years ago, last week, even five minutes ago — we are all learning all the time.

If a conflict situation arises now, you have a range of possible responses. Let's assume that there are five of them: A, B, C, D and E. (In most situations there are lots of possible responses, ranging from the likely to the extremely improbable).

Your previous experience, training and personal preferences mean that you will prefer certain options to others. This can be displayed as a graph.

Your options now

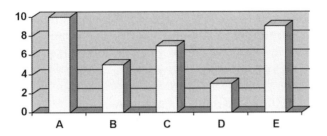

However, as you continue to learn and improve your skills these choices can change.

You may find that old options that were not very good can be removed (for example, if someone is angry with you, you becoming angry with them will generally make the situation worse). New options can be established. You might learn how to improve your rapport skills, so that in a conflict situation the other person finds it difficult to pursue the conflict because they find that they like you. Note that there will still be a root cause for the situation that needs to be dealt with, but conflict will no longer seem to be the way to do it.

So a new graph might look like this:

Your options now

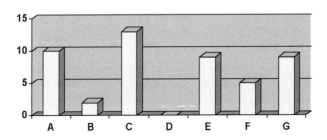

The new graph shows that option A has remained the same, B has reduced, C has grown, D has disappeared and E has remained the same. But there are two new options, F and G, which have added to your abilities to deal with a situation.

Obviously, it is up to you to decide which options work well and which don't, but an enquiring mind and paying attention to results will give you the clues you need. If something works, do more of it. If something doesn't work, do less or discard it completely.

Every conflict situation is unique and you shouldn't try to operate to a pre-set formula. However, every conflict is also similar and things that work once will probably work again. The secret to dealing with a situation is to pay attention and remain responsive.

Remember:

The more you know
and the more you can do,
the better are your chances
of succeeding

You are always learning

Make a list of five things that you have learnt in the last year. (These can be big things like learning to drive or to speak French, or small things like learning how to embolden text on the word processor or how to make pineapple upside-down cake.) It's easy to forget that you really do learn new things almost every day.

1. _____

2. _____

3. _____

4. _____

5. _____

Make a list of three things that you do more now than you did five years ago.

1. _____

2. _____

3. _____

Make a list of three things that you used to do that you now do less or not at all.

1. _____

2. _____

3. _____

REVISION TEST TWO

List the four rules of engagement.

1. _____

2. _____

3. _____

4. _____

Fill in the missing words.

"In any system of _____ beings or machines, the element in

that system with the _____ range of variability will be the

_____ element."

The more you _____ and the _____ you can

do, the _____ your chances of succeeding!

WHAT, WHY AND HOW

Words don't always mean what they say

The most important thing to pay attention to, when people are talking to you, is what they actually say. When they are angry, most people will try to explain what is causing the problem. But sometimes their anger may prevent them giving a clear explanation.

Other things that can hinder communications are a stutter or other speech impediment, a lack of vocabulary, other emotions (such as shyness and fear) and a lack of understanding of the subject matter.

Most people don't want to be angry, so by listening carefully and trying to understand their problem you have already started to deal with the anger.

The words that people say sometimes do not tell you what the problem is. This can be because the person is embarrassed or inarticulate, or assumes you know facts that you don't know.

Never be afraid to ask an angry person to explain what they want. Firstly, do it in a supportive manner. Secondly, explain to them that giving you the information that you require, will help you to help them. If you do these things, the majority of people will oblige.

WHAT DOES IT MEAN?

"Hello you old sod!"

may just mean

"Hello"

Alternatively

"Hello"

may really mean

"Hello you old sod!"

Another problem is that virtually all of us speak in jargon — technical jargon, business jargon, or just jargon based on real or assumed shared experiences. In a conflict situation, you must not use jargon yourself (as it may confuse and anger the other person), and you should politely ask the other person to explain the meaning of any jargon that they use.

Some people are straight-shooters — they say exactly what they mean. Others are not — they will circumvent the truth and present you with information that favours their point of view without necessarily being truthful. When dealing with conflict, stick to the truth. There is one exception to this rule — if someone physically threatens you, then it's okay to lie to them in order to make an escape.

WHY SHOULD YOU CARE?

Why should you care about the meaning of words that are spoken to you by someone who is being loud or angry or threatening?

The answer is simple.

1   It helps to resolve the situation

If you pay attention to people by listening to both the words they say and also considering the underlying meanings, then you will be able to communicate more efficiently and resolve situations faster.

It also shows that you care. Remember that being ignored angers people, so if you are paying attention to them you have already started trying to resolve the situation.

2   It makes your job easier

Most people want a job that is easy. It may be that we want a job that challenges us by being complicated or demanding of our expertise. However we still want to enjoy it as much as possible and to feel that we can cope.

Paying attention and learning to understand the meaning behind the words makes your job easier.

Sometimes when dealing with verbal aggression it may help to take notes. If you do, be sure to ask the other person for their permission to take notes. Explain that what they are saying is important and that you want to make sure that you understand what they are saying and the exact details of their problem.

Virtually anyone with an honest problem that is making them angry will appreciate the care and attention you are giving them.

3   It helps to keep you safe

An unresolved conflict situation can become physical. A badly resolved conflict situation may result in a complaint against you. So caring about the meaning of what is said can keep you safe.

It may not only be you. Someone whose verbal aggression is handled badly may come back and start on someone else in a worse manner. They might even become violent. If a colleague handles verbal aggression badly, it might be you who receives the visit from the person intent on using physical violence.

HOW CAN YOU TELL?

How can you understand the meaning behind the words?

List below some of the things that help you to know the meaning of what is said to you.

1. _____

2. _____

3. _____

There are five main ways of interpreting the meaning of what people say to us.

1   Content

What is actually said:

"Hello, how are you, it's lovely today."

is quite different from:

"Hey, you stupid idiot, come and deal with this now!"

It's easy to forget that most people actually mean (most of) what they say. Listen to people when they are being aggressive. Ignore bad language or personal attacks and focus on the information. That's where the reason for the aggression most often lies. Once you know what they want you can start to work on a solution to the problem.

When considering content, it is also important that you understand the words being used. If someone uses a word, phrase or term that you don't understand, politely interrupt and ask them to explain what they mean. If someone is very angry, it may be better not to interrupt but to wait until they pause. However do ask for clarification of anything that you don't understand.

EXAMPLE

Somebody comes up to you and says: "You must help me I'm being plagued by *Coccinella septempunctata*"

You might say: "I'm sorry, I want to help you, but I don't understand what you just said."

The person might say: "Ladybirds — you know those red coloured insects with the black spots — we have got thousands of them all over the place."

Whether you can or cannot help someone who is plagued by ladybirds is not the point — the point is that you now know what the problem is.

Another situation is where someone does not have the information you need.

EXAMPLE

Caller: "I'm ringing with a complaint. The goods you sent don't work and I want to return them."

You: "No problem, madam. Can you give me the reference number at the top of the delivery slip?"

Caller: "I didn't receive a delivery slip."

You: "No problem. Give me your postal code and I can look it up on the computer system."

Caller: "Thank you, it's xxx xxx"

In the above example, getting the required information was reasonably straightforward. Sometimes this will not be the case and you will need to be flexible and patient in order to resolve the problem.

2 Intonation

The tonal qualities of human speech vary enormously. The same word can be said in ways that indicate totally different meanings.

Try it for yourself.

Say "yes" in different ways so as to convey the following feelings: agreement, disagreement, scepticism, loathing, sarcasm, interest and lack of interest.

Do it now. Say "yes" aloud in a variety of different ways. Of course, if you are reading this book in a public place you may want to postpone this exercise until you get home or find somewhere private.

Then think of as many other feelings that may be shown in speech as you can.

If you can get a friend or colleague to help, this is an

amusing game. Try to say a word or phrase in as many different ways as you can and ask your partner to guess what meaning you are trying to convey. Then switch roles. Your partner says the word or phrase while you try and guess what they mean.

Try to improve your sensitivity, especially to things like mild annoyance or sarcasm. Both of these can be precursors of an outburst of real anger.

3   Body language

Is someone aggressive, menacing, happy, subdued, shifty, sad, honest, dishonest, open, friendly or potentially violent? A lot can be learned by observing body language. However, it's probably (for the non-specialist) the least reliable of all the indicators.

It's worth buying a book on the subject or attending a course, but remember that in the interpretation of body language there are myriad variables.

Someone who is talking to you has their arms crossed in front of their chest. They may be being defensive, they may be cold, they may have indigestion or they may just be comfortable in that position.

Hiding the mouth behind the hand when someone is speaking can indicate that they are lying. However, they might be embarrassed because they have ugly discoloured teeth.

Body language is useful and it is worth paying attention to, especially for indicators of extreme aggression.

EXAMPLE

A person is screaming at you and they are red in the face. If they continue to be angry but the colour leaves their face (they go pale), it can indicate that they are about to launch a physical attack.

This is because there is a biological process where the blood is shunted away from the surface of our skin just before we start to fight. So once the decision to fight has been made (and this may occur at a subconscious level) the colour of the face changes.

---

4 Circumstances

Your recognition of the circumstances that have caused a verbal conflict to take place should alert you to the meaning behind what people are saying. Do they feel frightened? Have they been hurt? Why are they upset? What has happened? These and other questions — which you should always ask yourself and may want to ask the other person — will give you the information that you need, in order to resolve the issue.

There are also physical circumstances. If you are working at a customer complaints desk, then it should be no surprise when a customer comes and complains.

Indeed, when you know that the circumstances put you in the firing line for verbal aggression, think of it as an advantage. You know in advance what is likely to happen and can marshal your forces — welcoming smile, calm persona, helpful tone of voice, and so on — to make the most of the advantage and to help you achieve a win-win resolution.

5 Experience

We all have experience — some more and some less. Trust your experiences and the experiences of others.

Learn from other people. Ask questions or watch how people with better conflict resolution skills handle things. Try to separate and identify the things they do that matter rather than the things they do that are superfluous or just personal habits. If you can do this it will be useful as you can take the benefits of experience without looking like a clone of someone else.

Make a list of people that you can ask for assistance, people who have more experience or different experience to yourself. These people can be real or (if you care to use your imagination) they can be fictitious. You can say to yourself: what would Fred do in this situation? Fred could be absolutely anyone who you feel might aid you — your Uncle Bill, Ronald Reagan, Sherlock Holmes, Luke Skywalker. This technique allows you to think 'outside the box' by pretending to be someone else. You allow your mind (especially the subconscious mind) the freedom to suggest methods that perhaps are not the ones that you normally consider.

List below some people (real or imaginary, known to you or not) that you think have good people handling skills, people who "know stuff".

1. _____

2. _____

3. _____

4. _____

5. _____

BODY LANGUAGE TEST

What might the following gestures mean?

1)   Arms crossed in front of body.

2)   Index finger pointing at your face.

3)   Not looking directly at you, being shifty.

4)   Listening with their head tipped to one side.

5)   Looking upwards towards the ceiling.

6)   Tapping on a tabletop with their finger while they are talking.

7)   Tapping on a tabletop with their finger while you are talking.

HOW TO DEAL WITH CONFLICT

Somebody comes up to you and says: "Now look here, you stupid fool, you promised me that my car would be fixed and ready by 11:00am, it's now 2:30pm and it's not fixed. What are you going to do about it?"

Now pretend that you are the assistant head of the service department that is responsible for fixing that car. Without worrying about specifics (things to do with the car), can you think of three fundamental strategies for dealing with this situation?

1. _____

2. _____

3. _____

The three main ways of dealing with verbal conflict are:

- Avoiding
- Deflecting
- Resolving

There may be other ways, but those are for you to discover.

Avoiding

Avoiding is the process of passing on an antagonistic person to someone else. "It's not my problem." "You need to call customer care." "Sorry, you've come to the wrong department." "You need to speak to my boss, can you come back tomorrow." These and thousands of similar responses are what you get from someone who is using avoidance so that they don't have to deal with aggression.

The advantages of avoidance are that it's quick, it requires minimum effort on your behalf and generally it's safe, as you are sending the aggressive person elsewhere.

A disadvantage is that it's unsatisfactory, both for the person being sent away and for you, as there is no feeling of completion or a job well done. Another disadvantage may be that it's inappropriate. Your job may be to deal with this person. Sending them away, although safeguarding yourself at that point in time, may cause a "career review meeting" because you are not handling the situation properly. You may even get the sack.

Think of the last time that you did this or that someone did this to you.

Deflecting

Deflecting could be called "elegant avoidance". It's the

process of getting rid of the problem while agreeing with the complainant. The conversation might include: "Oh that's terrible. I know just how you feel and I agree that you should be very upset by what has happened. Unfortunately, much as I'd like to help you, the only person who can deal with this matter is Mr Smith and he is away till tomorrow. If you call him then I am sure he will be able to help you."

You can see that the person seems to take the side of the complainant but in fact does nothing at all.

The advantages of deflection are that it's fairly quick and it's even safer than avoidance, because you are putting yourself on the same side as the aggressive person.

The disadvantages are that it's still unsatisfactory for the person being sent away and it still may be inappropriate behaviour for you.

Think of the last time that you did this or that someone did this to you.

Resolving

Resolving a situation when someone is being aggressive towards you can be difficult, but the rewards are great.

You will probably recognise the following as an example of something that has happened to you:

EXAMPLE

You ordered some goods, they have not been delivered when promised so you phone up the salesman who sold you them to see why they were late. The salesman says "Sorry but here in sales we have no way of checking despatch schedules." Just as you are thinking "Oh no", they go on to say, "But I will take your details and go and speak to Fred in shipping and I promise you that I will call you back within 20 minutes." All of a sudden you have a new friend, an advocate who is helping you deal with your problem. If they come back to you with a solution you feel great, and even if they cannot completely resolve the problem, you still (generally) feel grateful for their help and the extra information that they will have provided you with.

So be that person and take responsibility. Deal with the issues, or make sure that you get someone who is able to deal with the issues to do it. Check back to confirm that they did what you asked. If they are a superior or in another department, then still check back. It's corny but true: "If a job's worth doing it's worth doing well."

The advantages with this approach are that it's the safest, because you know whether the problem has been resolved or not. Also this is the one method that will give you true job satisfaction.

The disadvantages of this approach are that it takes time, needs commitment and requires you to be skilful, maybe even to develop skills that are not strictly part of your job description.

People

It's worth remembering that almost everybody you are ever going to meet is a good person — even that large, ugly, red-faced obscenity screaming "moron" who is threatening to rip your head off if you don't solve his problem now.

Generally, it is bad situations that create bad people.

Think back. Wasn't there a time when you lost your temper because of some set of circumstances? If someone had seen you at that moment and had to form a lasting impression of you, what would they think?

When resolving conflict situations, it often helps if you continually remind yourself that the other person could be you. How you do this will depend on your upbringing — you may have heard the phrases "Walk a mile in the other person's shoes", "Judge not, lest you be judged yourself" or "There but for the grace of God go I".

Everyone has an enormous range of emotions and behaviours and is capable of learning new ones and changing existing ones. The ugly red-faced obscenity screaming "moron" today may turn out to be your best friend (or your new boss) tomorrow.

REVISION TEST THREE

List the five basic ways that indicate the meaning
of what is said to us:

1. _____

2. _____

3. _____

4. _____

5. _____

List the three main ways of dealing with conflict:

1. _____

2. _____

3. _____

VERBAL SELF-DEFENCE

There are two categories of defensive methods that you can use to protect yourself from anger and hostile and abusive language.

The first category is **non-verbal techniques.** These techniques can be used even when you can't get a word in edgeways.

The second category is **verbal techniques**. These are the ones that you use to start to resolve the conflict situation.

Although the verbal techniques are generally the most important when it comes to resolving a conflict, it is the non-verbal techniques that give you the base (or it could be called the confidence) from which you can utilise the verbal techniques.

Non-verbal techniques

There are four non-verbal techniques that will allow you to exert a great deal of control in an aggressive situation. They are non-verbal so the other person, the aggressor, has no idea that you are doing anything — but their effect on both you and the aggressor can be truly amazing. They are:

- You don't know me
- Force-shield or bell jar
- You are like me
- Boundless love

Let's get you thinking

Choose one of the techniques listed above. Then write down what you think the technique is about and how it helps resolve a conflict situation.

_____

_____

_____

_____

_____

If you define the technique correctly, give yourself a pat on the back. If you describe a different meaning, you still deserve a pat on the back for being creative and thinking of a way to help yourself deal with aggression.

You don't know me

When people are being aggressive towards you, they will generally make assumptions about you based on what you represent. So if you are a civil servant they might say, "All you bureaucrats are alike, none of you care about ordinary people". But they don't know you and they don't know if you care or not — they are just making an assumption. However, in the heat of a conflict situation it is easy for you to fall into a variety of traps.

♦ Trap A. You start to deny their accusation and thus add to the conflict situation: "I do care", "No you don't", "Yes I do", "No you don't", and so on.

♦ Trap B. You start inwardly to agree with the accusation: "Oh, maybe I am a terrible person, maybe it's because I don't care that people are always being so nasty towards me."

♦ Trap C. You inwardly get angry with them and say to yourself: "What a stupid idiot. You won't get any help from me talking like that."

♦ Trap D. You mentally shut up shop: it's another lousy person causing you to have a lousy day in your lousy job.

The correct response is to remind yourself that the person who is being aggressive towards you does not know you. Indeed, if you stop and think about it for a moment you will realise that nobody ever knows anybody more than superficially. If we did know each other then how different the world would be — there would be far less anger and strife.

Force-shield or bell jar

The force-shield and bell jar techniques are ways you can protect yourself against a verbal attack, they are simple to learn and they really work.

Imagine that force-shields (the sort you see in science fiction movies) are a reality and that you are wearing a belt that contains a force-shield generator. When you activate it, it causes your skin to tingle slightly and you know that nothing can get through the force-shield to harm you. When someone starts being aggressive towards you, all you need to do is activate the force-shield and the aggression and the angry words just bounce off. Of course, after using the belt just a few times you will find that you have modified it so it works automatically, and any time anyone is aggressive towards you the force-shield snaps into place.

The bell jar technique is a variation on the force-shield. Imagine that you are inside a giant bell jar (a large dome-shaped cover made of very strong glass) and nobody and nothing can get to you. You are safe. If someone starts being aggressive, just imagine all that aggression bouncing off the thick glass wall that surrounds and protects you.

Some people have a problem when reading about force-shields and giant bell jars because they are not real. What we are actually doing is teaching our subconscious mind, via our conscious mind, that we want it to process information in a particular way. Once the subconscious learns what to do, aggression aimed towards us will simply be deflected away.

The conscious mind is happy to play games of make-believe, and the subconscious mind will treat the game as if it were real. The effect you get — of being automatically detached and protected from the anger aimed at you — is real. Try it and see for yourself.

In case you have any lingering doubts, then consider for a moment a fictional film that you have thoroughly enjoyed, one that has made you laugh or made you cry. Was it real? No, of course not. But your mind accepted the illusion without question.

This is a true story. Once on a training course I asked the attendees to role-play the force-shield and bell jar defences. One woman (who worked in a call centre) could not get the hang of them and said that she thought they were poor techniques. So I asked her what she did to protect herself from abusive calls. "Nothing," she said. I asked, "Really, you do nothing at all when someone is rude to you?" She then said, "Well, sometimes I do this", and showed how she would hold the phone at arms-length.

I smiled and explained to her and the rest of the attendees that what she did was exactly what I had asked them to do. Put distance between yourself and the offensive words so that they don't hurt you. It was very rewarding for me to see little light-bulbs switching on in people's heads as they realised how easy it was to do these things.

You are like me

When people are in conflict, they generally focus on the differences. In order not to be in conflict, focus on the similarities.

This exercise is one that you can do whenever you meet someone, on a bus, train or anywhere you can see people.

Look for the ways in which they are similar to you. Are they driving the same car, or the same colour car? Do they wear the same colour shoes as you? Are you both wearing a watch, or do you both stand with most of your weight on your right leg? It doesn't matter what the connection is, but you will start to train yourself to see those connections. Maybe it's that you are the same sex, or the same height, or they have a child with them. You think to yourself: "Yes, they are like me. I'm a parent too."

What's the purpose? It will make you more observant (which is a good thing to be, for safety reasons). You will start to pay more attention to people (remember what I said earlier about how people can become angry if ignored). You will also start to see that other people are just like you, and that will make you more sympathetic to their situation.

Also, being sympathetic will help you when you interact with others. You will still take any required action or follow any required procedures, but it will affect and improve the way you communicate with them.

EXAMPLE

Someone walks up to you in the street and asks you to give them money for "something to eat". You can say "Yes" with a smile on your face and the thought going through your mind "What a shame that this person needs to beg, how lucky I am to be able to afford to help them", or you can say "Yes" but be thinking "What a worthless person, I'd better give them some money or otherwise they may become angry and threaten me".

Alternatively, you can say "No". You could say it with a scowl on your face and the thought going through your mind "what a worthless person", or you can say "no" with a pleasant yet firm demeanour and think "what an unfortunate person".

Either way, can you also see how a good thought is better than a bad one?

In case you can't, I'll explain. If you do something with a bad thought then those feelings stay within you and cause stress (only slight but it's cumulative) and negativity to build up. If there are some residual bad feelings about another matter, they can affect the next conversation you have with someone. Think of people who have a bad day at the office and then go home and have an argument. This can be caused by residual bad feelings.

Boundless love

It helps if you once owned a puppy or a kitten or have been the parent of an infant or have seen an exceptional sunrise — something that made you feel an outpouring of love. I'm not talking about sexual love, or even romantic love, but selfless, boundless love.

Next time someone is being aggressive towards you, just try and recapture inside yourself that feeling of boundless love. You will then find yourself responding to them from that very positive state rather than a state of annoyance or anger.

Of course, this technique is difficult and needs a lot of practice. It makes sense to start with minor situations rather than trying to defuse a mindless axe-wielding psychopath with a loving smile.

However, the practice will pay off and you will find that something very strange happens. You will get into fewer arguments; people will behave better towards you; and even if they occasionally don't, you won't mind it nearly so much.

Non-verbal techniques – summary

Generally, non-verbal techniques are short-term stop-gap methods to allow you to remain composed in the face of sudden verbal aggression. Once you know that you are safe, you need to look at ways of helping yourself and the other person and defusing the situation.

Verbal techniques

There are four verbal techniques that you need to learn.

- Following and leading
- Asking intelligent questions
- Wanting to help
- Taking control

Let's get you thinking

Choose one of the above four techniques and write down what you think the technique is about and how it helps resolve a conflict situation.

As before, the object of the exercise is to get your mind thinking about ways to deal with aggression.

Following and leading

Have you ever been in a situation where you are talking to someone who has a pronounced regional or foreign accent and you find that you are speaking in a similar way? It's quite common.

When you are following speech patterns you are talking to a person using a similar rhythm, volume and tonality to theirs.

Imagine you want to tune in to an FM radio station. Could you pick up the transmission if your radio was set to AM? Obviously not. So if someone is being loud and aggressive, can you communicate with them by being quiet? Well, sometimes you can but more often you can't. Your being quiet just makes them more angry because you seem (to them) to be unsympathetic.

However, being loud and aggressive yourself will just make the situation worse. So what's the answer? The answer is to be loud (but not quite as loud as them) to match the speech rhythm, but to remain calm and friendly.

By matching the tone and (some of) the volume you build rapport — your radio is tuned to the same wavelength — and they will then be able to hear you. Once you have followed then you can lead. Once you have rapport you can suggest to someone, often by simply altering your tone and volume, that they should alter theirs. Also (if the circumstances allow) you can suggest a change of venue or position. "Let's sit down and talk about this", or "Let's go and discuss this over a cup of coffee".

Asking intelligent questions

In many conflict situations there is a need to ask questions: "What is the matter?", "What is the reference number on the letter that was sent to you?", and so on.

There are two ways you can ask a question — one of them is intelligent and the other is not.

EXAMPLE

Suppose you are working in a call centre where people phone in with requests for a visit by a maintenance engineer to fix a domestic appliance. You need to confirm that they have a maintenance contract, the type of appliance, their address, and so on. You also need some basic information about the fault so you can make an appointment for an engineer to call. Simple.

The phone rings.

You: "Call centre, how may I help you?"
Them: "I was telling someone that my fridge is broken and I got cut off."
You: "Contract reference number please."
Them: "Can you send an engineer right away?"
You: "I need your reference number, please."
Them: "I gave all my details before, I just want an engineer."
You: "Please give me your reference number."
Them: "Is that all you can say? What are you, a bloody recording?"

As you can see this isn't going terribly well.

Let's try again.

You: "Call centre, how may I help you?"
Them: "I was telling someone that my fridge is broken and I got cut off"
You: "I'm sorry to hear that, can you please give me your contract reference number so I can look up your details on the computer and then we can organise an engineer to come and fix it."
Them: "It's reference number 12345678"

Isn't that better? The trick is to ask questions in such a way that they also include the reason why the question is being asked and explaining the benefit of compliance. In the example, the reason is to "look up your details" and the benefit "organise an engineer".

Start listening to conversations, yours and other people's, and you will be amazed how often people take things for granted and don't explain why they are asking questions.

If you have a credit card and you phone up the credit card company with a query, they often say: "For security reasons can you give me your mother's maiden name?" That is an intelligent question. Imagine that the first time you phoned the company a terse voice asked: "What's your mother's maiden name?" What would you think? You would probably be quite annoyed about being asked to disclose personal information. But the opening statement "for security reasons" makes the question sensible, friendly and intelligent.

Wanting to help

Many people are shy and do not tell people how they feel. Too many people live difficult lives and do not get the care that they deserve. You will be pleased to know that just a few words can make life better for others and for you.

If there is a conflict situation, saying "I do want to help you" can be enormously powerful. It doesn't mean that you will be able to help them (that depends on the circumstances) but that you do want to.

Sometimes we forget to say it, assuming that the other person will know that we want to help them. The truth is that the other person may misunderstand and feel that you don't care about them. Take the time, make the effort to actually say "I do want to help you".

Taking control

Sometimes it can seem as if you can only stop someone being aggressive either by giving in or by trying to placate them. However, in many situations the exact opposite is required and you need to take control.

EXAMPLE

Someone is behaving petulantly and being loud and aggressive. Your intuition and experience tell you that trying to be reassuring or calming or trying to reason is not going to work (or maybe you have already tried this and it hasn't worked). In a firm and commanding tone, direct the person to do what you need them to do, and explain both the disadvantage to them if they don't comply and the advantage to them if they do.

EXAMPLE

They say loudly: "You stupid idiot."

You say: "Please lower your voice and speak politely or else I will have you removed. If you treat me with respect then I am willing to help you and am sure that we can sort this problem out."

You can see that although you are in command, this does not imply censure of the person. You are stating that you are willing to help them if they help you. Most people — even when they are angry — are still able to listen to reason.

REVISION TEST FOUR

List two ways in which you can deal with verbal aggression (without saying a word).

1. _____

2. _____

Now think of a new way (something not in this book) that you can do, to deal with aggression (without saying a word).

1. _____

List two verbal techniques that will help you deal with conflict.

1. _____

2. _____

Now think of a new way (something not in this book) that you can say, to help you deal with aggression.

1. _____

BAD LANGUAGE

A simple idea under-pins my approach to dealing with people whose language might otherwise be considered rude, uncouth or offensive:

#!!$#
#<!<%#!#

remember that just as static and interference may garble an otherwise sensible radio message, so anger and bad language can do the same for a verbal message.

Also, remember it's not the speaking of 'bad language' that is offensive — it is merely a collection of sounds. It is the person who hears that language who determines its meaning and who decides if it is offensive or not.

If I say "Hi" to an English-speaking person they will think it is a greeting. If I say "Hi" to a Cantonese-speaking person they may think that I am very rude. Cantonese uses six tones, and saying "Hi" in a particular tone is an extremely coarse term for the vagina. (If you want to learn to swear in Cantonese you will have to carry out your own research.)

English is a **living** language that is constantly altering. Individuals, **groups**, technical and social change, all are continually influencing its growth and development.

If I call you stupid, it may be an insult or it may be an accepted greeting within our social group. A person speaking to you may well (when being aggressive) utilise the speech patterns he is most familiar with, even if he normally moderates them in general conversation. We need to be able to defuse verbal aggression and not add to a situation by allowing another person's language to trigger inappropriate emotions.

Think about words that annoy, anger or upset you. List three of them below (or on a separate sheet of paper) and then write down why they affect you. An example might be the word "fatty", and the reason could be "because I am not comfortable with my present weight and shape".

If you are uncomfortable with writing down a swear-word, just refer to it as "the f word" or "the c word" or whatever.

Try to be very specific about why the word offends you.

1) Word:

    Reason:

2) Word:

    Reason:

3) Word:

    Reason:

Rude words

There are numerous words that can be used in an insulting or aggressive manner.

The interesting thing about the English language is that any word can have its meaning changed by usage, or by intent.

Many of the more common swear-words can be used factually, or to express surprise or annoyance, or as an insult.

The word "fuck" is great for this.

PHRASE	MEANING
"Well, fuck me."	Indicating surprise
"Fuck off."	Expressing anger
"That's fucking brilliant."	Expressing approval

A word can have an immense variety of meanings.

Choose a word (a swear-word or any ordinary word) and list several possible ways it can be used.

WORD	MEANING

Spelling

Shakespeare wrote in *Romeo and Juliet,* "What's in a name? That which we call a rose by any other name would smell as sweet". It is true that a word is just a name for a thing, not the thing itself. But strangely, where swear-words are concerned we allow the word itself to take on power. To help show just how trivial and fragile words are, try the following exercise.

In the first column write down a swear-word, and in the second column find a word that is spelt almost exactly the same apart from one or two letters. If someone swears at you, just mentally change the letters.

Here are a few to get you started:

BAD WORD	GOOD WORD
BUGGER	*BIGGER*
SHIT	*SHOT*
QUEER	*CHEER*

Now it's your turn.

If you found that there were words that you couldn't change in a maximum of two letters, it doesn't matter. Just playing this word game lets you see that you are in command. The words do not control you, you control them.

The tonality and the person's body language often indicate whether a swear-word is being used as a weapon or is merely a strange form of punctuation.

I remember a lovely cartoon. Paddington Bear is walking along and then he stubs his toe. "Treetops," he yelps. Then he looks shamefaced towards the reader and says, "Sometimes 'Marmalade' just isn't enough."

You see for Paddington "Marmalade" was a rude word and "Treetops" was even worse.

Rudeness or abuse is mainly to do with intent, not content. If I call you a shit or tell you to fuck off, it's not the words that matter, it's the emotion that powers them. What generally upsets us is the aggression (or other emotion) behind the words.

Think about this. If it were the word itself, then every time you heard it, it would be equally as bad, whether or not the word was aimed at you. But be honest, if you see a TV play where someone swears, it is not as personally offensive or as threatening as when someone swears at you. So the question is, how do you remove any negative effects when someone swears at you?

If someone swears at you

How you respond to an insult is up to you. You can take it to heart and let it annoy, upset and injure you. Or you can interpret what is happening — someone wants to communicate with you and they don't yet know how to use the right words to elicit your help.

Just say to yourself:

"If you swear at me, I will treat it as an invitation to communicate and a request for my help."

Also, never forget the childhood litany:

"Sticks and stones may break my bones, but words will never hurt me."

You think that's corny? It is, but it's true if you make it so.

THE TELEPHONE

The telephone is a fantastic invention and we can (most of the time) talk to people around the world as easily as if they were next door.

This is great until a problem occurs and an argument starts, then the telephone can cause some special problems.

However, the good news is that it also has some special advantages too.

We'll start with the good news.

Good news

- ◆   They don't know you

- ◆   They can't hurt you

- ◆   You can always hang up

Let's get you thinking

Choose one of the above three techniques and write down what you think the technique is about and how it can help you resolve a conflict situation.

If you define the technique correctly, give yourself 10 points. If you describe a different meaning, you still deserve 10 points for being creative and thinking of a way to help yourself deal with aggression.

They don't know you

The telephone is a means of communication that carries with it (for most people) a strong sense of "knowing" the person on the other end of the line. This is because we are used to the technology, feel comfortable with this method of communication and can often create vivid mental pictures of the person to whom we are talking.

However, this picture is extremely imprecise, and when someone is angry the picture they have of you (as an evil, ugly, uncaring monster) is false.

You need to keep reminding yourself that the "you" they are talking to is their "you" not the real "you". So when they make assumptions about you like "You aren't listening", "You don't care", "All you people are alike", it's not actually you.

The problem is that all too often we buy into their "you" language and mentally (and sometimes verbally) start responding with "you" language of our own. This may be by thinking "You stupid person, listen to what I'm saying" or "You are such an idiot to be complaining about such a trivial matter". You can see that "you" language can be contagious.

So remember that a voice on the phone isn't the whole person and allow a little leeway for the "you" effect.

They can't hurt you

In cartoons, the hand leaps out of the telephone and hits the person on the head with a big hammer. That doesn't happen in real life, of course.

Remember that however much someone screams and shouts at you on the phone, they cannot (at that moment) hurt you, so you can remain calm and in control.

However, don't use the fact that someone cannot hurt you as an excuse to be rude. You don't want people complaining to your employer, or even worse coming round to your office to "sort you out".

You can always hang up

If someone is continuously rude or abusive and you feel that you cannot get them to modify their behaviour, then you may need to hang up.

There are a variety of ways you can do this. My preferred method is as follows.

EXAMPLE

Caller: "Blah blah blah blah blah."

You: "Please stop using that sort of language, I am sorry that you are upset but when you are rude to me I find it hard to concentrate on your problem and I do want to help you."

Caller: "I'll talk anyway I bloody like, you stupid idiot."

You: "Please, if you carry on being rude I will have to terminate this conversation."

Caller: "Who the bloody hell do you..."

You: (interrupting) "Bye Bye."

You immediately hang up and in a work environment log the call and your action.

The caller may well call back. If they then modify their behaviour, you can help them; if not, simply refuse to deal with them while they are being abusive.

Most people will learn the lesson very quickly and will modify their behaviour if they want to talk to you.

Bad news

- They can't see you care
- They may not hear the meaning of your words
- Distance

Let's do some more thinking

I know that you may want to skip this exercise, but take the time and do it. It will pay dividends.

Choose one of the above three techniques and write down what you think the technique is about and how it helps resolve a conflict situation.

Hopefully that wasn't too onerous. Well done if you defined the technique correctly and congratulations if you were creative in thinking of a way to help yourself deal with aggression.

They can't see you care

Most people use sight as their primary sense. On the phone you are deprived of the huge amount of visual information that is received in a face-to-face conversation. So if you are saying to someone "I want to help you", all they have to go on is your words and your tone of voice. Statistics vary, but about 70% of communication is visual. As this cannot readily be done (yet) via a telephone line, your words need to be very clear and your tonality very convincing.

If you get the words or the tonality wrong, it will be almost impossible to convince an angry person that you want to help them, or even to make them believe that you are listening. "You aren't listening to me" is a frequently heard complaint.

They may not hear the meaning of your words

Just as you can't be seen, you can't see the person on the other end of the line. So you can't easily tell if they understand what you are saying.

It's also easy for the words to be heard — "I want to help you" — but the meaning — "I really do want to help you" — to be lost. They may hear the words but not understand the meaning.

There is not much that you can do about this, because in order to find out if the other person understands you will need to ask questions. But if someone is angry, they may get fed up with being questioned and misinterpret the questions as evidence of either your stupidity or your condescending attitude, which is not what you want at all.

The best advice is to try and avoid jargon, speak clearly, and try and maintain a friendly tone of voice.

Distance

The telephone makes people sound close, but physically they are apart. It's worth remembering that distance does make communication difficult. So sometimes the appropriate response is to say to an angry caller, "Let's meet". Of course, if the caller is very angry, you may want to arrange the meeting a couple of days ahead to let them cool down. This is a judgement you must make as some people will calm down whereas others will simmer and come to the boil just in time for the meeting. If you think the person is going to simmer, the sooner you meet them the better.

Types of telephone calls

When making or receiving a telephone call always remember the basics:

- Smile as you pick up the handset — it alters your tonality, making you sound friendly.

- Say who you are, ideally give your first name — giving your name implies trust and makes you a person rather than just an anonymous voice.

- Listen without interrupting, and don't cut in because you assume that you know what is being said.

- Ask for clarification or extra information if there is something you don't understand.

- Be polite, even if the other person is being rude — maintain a kind and professional attitude.

We shall consider four types of call. They need to be handled in slightly different ways in order to resolve conflict as swiftly as possible.

- Abusive

- Pathetic

- Angry

- Unintelligible

By the way, 'Pathetic' is defined as "having a capacity to move one to either compassionate or contemptuous pity" (Source Merriam-Webster dictionary). I am using it in the compassionate sense where you are dealing with someone who is in genuine hardship and you feel sorry for them.

Abusive calls

An abusive call is one where the person is talking calmly but either swears a lot or talks to you in an insulting manner.

The way to handle this type of call is to:

- ◆ Know your rights
- ◆ Remember it's not "you"
- ◆ Be polite
- ◆ Take control

Know your rights

Nobody has the right to be rude or abusive towards you. If you cannot gain control of the conversation and get the caller to speak politely to you then you may want to terminate the conversation.

Remember it's not "you"

The caller doesn't know you. You are just a person on the end of a phone who represents whatever organisation (or problem) the caller is unhappy with.

Be polite

Always be polite. Keep your temper (and your sense of humour) and you will be able to deal with the caller more efficiently.

Take control

Tell the caller what you want them to do and why, if they do it, it will be beneficial to them.

EXAMPLE

"Mr Smith, please stop swearing at me. If you keep on swearing then I will terminate this call. However, if you treat me reasonably then I will be delighted to help you resolve this problem."

Other actions

Trust your instincts ("Use the force, Luke") and be alert to anything that will help you to resolve the conflict.

Pathetic calls

A pathetic call is one where the caller has a genuine problem and is in genuine distress. For some reason you feel drawn to them and sympathetic to their needs.

To handle this type of call:

◆ Try to care
◆ Don't get personally involved
◆ Be polite
◆ Take control

Try to care

It's good to care about people. You need to be safe and you shouldn't get too involved, but caring is good.

Don't get personally involved

You will generally do no good by getting too involved with a pathetic situation. However, it is your choice and you might choose to get involved.

EXAMPLE

Caller: "I can't pay the bill because I have no money."

You: "Don't worry, I understand your situation, I will pay the bill for you."

If you were to do this (and of course it is your right as a human being to do so if you wish) you would be solving the caller's problem but you would be doing so personally rather than professionally.

A professional approach to the same problem might be:

Caller: "I can't pay the bill because I have no money."

You: "Don't worry, I understand your situation, and the solution is simple. The company can offer you credit terms so you can spread your payments over the next six months."

Be polite

Always, always, always be polite. It costs so little but is often the key to resolving a dispute.

Take control

Taking control is less important with a pathetic call than with an abusive call, but you will still need to establish facts and perhaps give instructions. Be firm, but be polite.

Other actions

Trust your instincts ("Use the force, Luke") and be alert to anything that will help you to resolve the conflict.

Note that 'Other actions' is repeated in each situation because you and your ability to resolve conflict are the most important points. This book is your guide, not your master.

Angry calls

An angry caller may also be an abusive caller. The problem with angry callers is that often the anger is in control. They may not be completely logical in their demands or in the way that they interpret what you say. The way to handle this type of call is to:

◆ Acknowledge the anger

◆ Try to be helpful

◆ Take control

◆ Be polite

Acknowledge the anger

Tell the caller that you can hear that they are angry and that you want to help them. You may want to say that you 'understand' why they are angry, but only do this if they have explained their problem to you and you do really 'understand'. Otherwise you may come across as being patronising, which will not help resolve the situation.

Try to be helpful

Tell the caller that you want to help them. Saying that you want to help does not mean that you will be able to help, but it shows that your intentions are good.

Take control

Tell the caller what you can do for them and what they need to do in order to get your help.

Be polite

I know it can be difficult — but it really is an important part of the solution.

"Mrs Smith, I am sorry that you are angry and I do want to help you. Please tell me exactly what happened to your car and then I will be able to route your call to the correct person."

In this example, the first thing that is said is "I am sorry". This does not imply guilt or responsibility for the caller's problem, just that you care about them. Then "you are angry", which specifically acknowledges the anger and allows the caller (even if only at a subconscious level) to realise that you are paying attention to them. Then "I do want to help you", which again illustrates to the caller that you are on their side, even though you may or may not be able to help them. It is your attitude that matters). "Please tell me exactly..." is where you start to take control in order to elicit the information that you need.

Obviously, throughout the example the language has been polite and helpful.

Other actions

"Once more unto the breach", says King Henry in Act III Scene 1 of Shakespeare's *Henry V*. In other words, continue to trust your instincts, your intuitions, your experience and your understanding that conflict resolution requires continued flexibility of thought, word and action.

Unintelligible calls

With a bit of luck you won't have to deal with unintelligible calls too often because they are very demanding. A call may be unintelligible for a variety of reasons. It could be:

◆ Someone who is unable to speak clearly as they are overcome by emotion.

- ◆ Someone with a speech problem, such as a severe stutter.

- ◆ Someone who speaks with a strong accent or in a foreign language.

In these cases as in the others the procedure is the same:

- ◆ Try to be helpful
- ◆ Take control
- ◆ Be polite
- ◆ Get help

Try to be helpful

Even if the caller doesn't understand what you are saying, (which may or may not be the case), your tone of voice will convey the fact that you are trying to help.

Take control

The caller may or may not respond, but your priority is to try to establish what the problem is. If you have ever had to dial 999 (or 911), you will probably remember how good the emergency operator was at taking control of the conversation.

Be polite

The same as trying to be helpful — your tone will carry even if the content does not.

Get help

If you can't communicate then all you can do is to try to get help. The mechanism for getting help will, of course, depend on the circumstances in which you are taking the call.

Other actions

Yes, our old friend still applies — trust your instincts and be alert.

REVISION TEST FIVE

On the telephone the good news is:

1. _____

2. _____

3. _____

and the bad news is:

1. _____

2. _____

3. _____

List the four types of telephone call.

1. _____

2. _____

3. _____

4. _____

Think of one new thing that you might do to deal with
aggression on the telephone:

_____

_____

FACE-TO-FACE

It is always most important to be aware that a face-to-face meeting is potentially more dangerous than a telephone call.

Make certain that you act and react appropriately.

Types of face-to-face meetings

There are two simple rules to remember when in a face-to-face meeting.

1. Always consider your own safety as the main priority. It is easy to forget that an angry person may become physically violent.

81

So what would happen if someone exhibits signs that show they are about to get violent? Can you escape? Can you call for help? What options do you have?

2.　　　Always try to resolve situations verbally and immediately. The quicker you can resolve a conflict situation, the sooner you can move on. More importantly, the sooner the situation is resolved, the better are your chances of safety, a happy "client" and preservation of your own peace of mind.

There are various types of meetings. Each will require slightly different methods to handle them optimally:

- Upset
- Pathetic
- Angry
- Threatening violence

Upset meeting

An upset meeting is a meeting with someone who is distressed and showing obvious signs of emotional upheaval.

The rules for dealing with someone who is upset are:

- Remain calm
- Take control
- Elicit facts

Remain calm

If you become agitated or upset, you will not be in the best frame of mind to deal with the real issues.

Important points to remember:

◆ Be uninvolved and dispassionate about any negative comments about yourself, your organisation, or its products or services.

◆ Use straightforward explanations in plain English. Avoid jargon wherever possible and when it is necessary, always explain it.

◆ Be friendly but not too personal. People who are upset may misinterpret a casual remark.

Take control

It will probably be necessary for you to establish facts, obtain information or explain options or procedures. In order to do this you need to communicate with knowledge and authority while listening to the other parties' opinions.

Elicit facts

Find out why the person is upset. Find out what they want and need in order to deal with the situation. Find out as much as you can.

Explain that in order to help them you need this information. Be polite, and always pay attention to what they say.

It may help if you have a notepad and ask permission to take notes. You can say: "I'd like to take notes of what you say so that we can both be sure that I understand the issues." The majority of people will be impressed by your professionalism and pleased that you consider them important enough to record their point of view.

If you take notes, it is also a good idea to stop from time-to-time and ask for clarification, and to check that your notes are accurate.

Notes are an aid to memory, so you should not try to write down everything they say. It will not serve any useful purpose and may indeed hinder your ability to understand the issues. It is also likely to diminish the rapport between you as you will be (in effect) ignoring them.

Pathetic meeting

A pathetic meeting is a meeting with someone who is in a position that you feel sympathy with.

EXAMPLE

If you were a single parent and you worked as a benefits officer, you might feel sympathy with the plight of someone who was also a single parent. Maybe their partner has just died, or they have no money, or they find that the benefits process is too slow to help them, and so on.

In this case you might be personally drawn into their case and feel a need to intervene at a personal level.

The rules in this situation are:

- Try to care
- Don't get personally involved
- Be polite
- Take control

Try to care

It's a good thing to care about people. Even if it sometimes makes the situation more stressful (for you), it will help you to find a solution. It is far better to care and be motivated than to be detached and just be "doing the job".

Don't get personally involved

Note that if you want to get personally involved — in this example by taking money out of your own wallet and giving it to them — you may believe this is a good thing and it is certainly your right. However, when resolving a conflict situation, you need to maintain appropriate boundaries and remain focused on the solution. If you get involved this may prove difficult.

Be polite

It is very easy to talk down to people who are suffering from genuine hardship or are distressed. Try and be considerate, polite and professional.

Angry meeting

An angry meeting is a meeting where the person you are dealing with is losing control. Their physical and verbal actions will be undisciplined and they may be loud. They may use bad language and they may make (verbal) personal attacks.

The main things to do in this type of meeting are:

- Acknowledge the anger
- Try to be helpful
- Take control
- Be polite
- Be careful

Acknowledge the anger

Anger often embarrasses or frightens us so we don't mention it. It is much better to show the angry person that you recognise they are angry.

It is acceptable to say: "I'm terribly sorry that you are angry, I sympathise and ...."

Try to be helpful

Tell the angry person that you want to help them. This shows that you are paying attention to them and are on their side.

You can say: "I'm terribly sorry that you are angry, I sympathise and I do want to help you ...."

Take control

If someone is angry, either their manner may be getting in the way of you finding a solution to their problem, or they may be disrupting your workplace. Take control in a way that clearly shows them that by modifying their behaviour, they will benefit.

You can say: "I'm terribly sorry that you are angry, I sympathise and I do want to help you. Please help me by taking the time to sit down and explain to me the problem so that I can help resolve it."

Be polite

When someone is angry, in almost all cases it helps to be polite. It is easy but generally incorrect, to go into school-teacher mode and say: "Be quiet, acting like that won't help you at all" or "If you don't talk politely then I won't help you". It is much better to refrain from judgement and not be adversarial or dictatorial.

Remember a time when you lost your temper or were angry. Would you not have preferred people to talk to you in an intelligent and polite manner?

There are exceptions to every rule. There is definitely one to the "polite" rule. Some people are bullies, and when they become angry, they interpret politeness as weakness and it just makes them more angry. If you are dealing with someone like this, then after trying the normal strategy (that will work with most people) you may need to go into school-teacher mode and say something like:

"Stop talking like that. Your behaviour is not acceptable. Sit down now." And (sometimes) they will turn from a raging lion into a little lamb. However, remember to be careful.

Be careful

Whenever you are face-to-face with someone there is always the potential for physical violence. One of the primary aims of verbal conflict management is to prevent physical violence. You must continually monitor the situation and be ready to adjust your strategy or to terminate a meeting if you feel unable to deal with it.

Threatening violence meeting

If a specific verbal threat is made along the lines of:

- ◆   "I'm going to smash your face in"
- ◆   "I'm going to kill you"
- ◆   "I'm going to hit you"

and you believe that the person making this threat is serious in their intent, you should immediately consider terminating the meeting and leaving. However, while making your exit, or if for some reason leaving is not an option, the verbal resources to consider are:

- ◆   Take control (without being adversarial)
- ◆   Acknowledge the mood
- ◆   Be careful
- ◆   Calm it down

Take control

Say in a firm voice: "I can appreciate that you are very upset and I do want to help you but you must realise that I can't do anything if I am scared. Can we both calm down and try and sort this out."

You see how there is no suggestion of blame, and there is no school-teacher type comment, such as "You must behave properly or else ..." which could make matters worse.

Focus on what you want in terms of a positive outcome and supportive behaviour.

Acknowledge the mood

In English you cannot safely acknowledge a specific threat.

EXAMPLE

Angry person says: "I'm going to punch you."

You say: "Oh, so you are going to punch me, are you?"
or   "Punch me?"
or   "You're not going to punch me."
or   "How dare you threaten to punch me."
or even   "Ha ha ha — punch me."

Any response that includes specific mention of the threatened action, such as the statements above (and any others that you can think of), make that action much more likely to happen.

What you must do instead is to focus on and acknowledge the underlying mood.

You might say: "I'm sorry that you are so upset, I do want to help you." or "I'm sorry that you are angry, I do want to help you." Focus on the emotion that the person is feeling and immediately state that you want to help them. Generally, we do not become violent with people who are helping us.

Be careful

Since a threat has been made and since the person is obviously angry, try to be vigilant in case they try to assault you. Be prepared to get away. Also try to give the person some extra space. Generally, the angrier someone is, the more space they will want to claim as their own. So being a normal distance from someone who is angry will feel invasive to them and may increase aggression or even (in their mind) be the trigger that provokes an assault.

Calm it down

Use any method that you can think of to calm things down. Suggest taking a break; explain that you can only help if things are peaceful; suggest that you go and get a drink (preferably water or a fizzy drink, not anything hot that could be thrown at you).

Keeping an outward veneer of calmness yourself (even though you may be shaking like a leaf in a storm on the inside) may well be helpful.

Other actions

Since a physical threat has been made, anything that is within the law, absolutely anything, is permissible.

Suppose you work for social services and when visiting someone's home they become angry because you can't arrange for their elderly parent to go to a day-care centre. They get so angry they say "I'm going to get my gun and shoot you!"

Make an excuse to leave: "Hold on, I can get you what you want. I've just realised that if we fill in a form J-165 then I can get your parent fast-tracked into the day-care centre early next week. I've got one in my car; I'll just get the form and be right back." Once out, you get into your car and drive off.

Was there such a thing as a 'form J-165'? No.

Did you lie? Yes.

Was it necessary in order to keep you safe? Yes.

In simple terms, your safety comes first. Nobody has the right to threaten you. If they do, then you should do whatever is necessary for your own self-preservation.

REVISION TEST SIX

What is the most important thing to remember
about a face-to-face meeting?

List the four types of face-to-face meeting.

1.

2.

3.

4.

List the four things to do if someone threatens physical violence.

1.

2.

3.

4.

OBSERVATIONS

With verbal aggression management, you have to be constantly aware that you are dealing with an art, not a science. There are some important points that you should always remember:

- With people there are no certainties.
- Learn from your mistakes.
- Learn from your successes.
- Keep an open mind.
- Do your best.
- Have fun.

With people there are no certainties

If you think of a science, say mathematics, then when you add up 2 and 2 you get the number 4, not occasionally, not sometimes, but always. Because maths is a science and precise 2 + 2 = 4 is always true.

With people it can be quite different. Sometimes 2 + 2 equals 4, but other times it's 3 or 7, or it just doesn't add up at all. In other words, people are infinitely variable. We are all different from each other and we all change day by day, moment by moment. There are general trends and some more or less predictable responses. However always remember that there are no guarantees when dealing with people — especially people who are angry.

Learn from your mistakes

If you do something and it doesn't work, then change it. During an encounter with someone who is aggressive you need to be on your toes and paying attention to the strategies that you use. If something you do does not calm the situation down or help you move towards resolution, then abandon it and try something else. After an encounter, think back and try to decide what you could have done differently and better.

Learn from your successes

When you do something correctly (or if you see someone else do something successfully), learn from that success. Think about the specific actions that made it successful, and try to think of ways to make it an even more effective strategy the next time you use it.

Keep an open mind

Try not to make judgements about people or the situations that they are in. If you have judged someone and found them to be lacking, you may find yourself thinking:

"It's their own fault."
"People like them always ..."

"You are stupid, why can't you understand what I'm explaining."

This type of thinking will get in the way of resolving the situation. Ignore everything except what you have to do to reach a solution. Be ruthless in the most friendly way.

Be open to new ideas and methods that can help you deal with aggressive people. Research is continually turning up new facts and new methods. A little bit of research may make your life a lot easier.

Do your best

Sometimes you will be bored, or tired, or coming down with a cold, or you may find that you are dealing with someone that you simply don't like.

In these cases (and in others), you have to take control of yourself and resolve to do your best. You will find that simply making that decision will change the way you think and work and the results you get. It's corny but true that people with a positive attitude generally do better. It's the attitude that creates the success, not (as some people think) the other way around.

Have fun

Enjoy your work, enjoy your life and have fun. Find new ways to enjoy things. You can be creative and look for the irony or the absurdness, the good or the humorous in every situation. Do whatever it takes to make your work and your life enjoyable. You owe it to yourself and it will have a profound effect on your ability to deal with people who are aggressive.

Final thoughts

In any interaction between people there are an infinite number of possible outcomes, and as every individual is unique, there are no guarantees as to outcomes.

So keep it simple:

◆   Do your best to be friendly to everyone.

◆   Do your best to be understanding.

◆   Do your best to learn as much as you can.

◆   Do your best to listen to the other person.

But what (you may ask) if the best is not good enough? In that case relax and remember that you can only do your best. The rest is in the hands of (depending on your beliefs and maybe unknown but absolute truths) divine providence, natural laws, sheer damn luck or fairies at the bottom of the garden.

Until next time ...

FURTHER READING

Title: *Verbal Judo*
Author: George J. Thompson
            ISBN: 0-688-13786-5

Title: *The Complete Idiot's Guide to Verbal Self-Defence*
Author: Lillian Glass
            ISBN: 0-02-862741-5

Title: *Key Concepts in Language and Linguistics*
Author: R. L. Trask
            ISBN: 0-415-15742-0

Title: *Assert Yourself*
Author: Gael Lindenfield
            ISBN: 0-7225-2652-0

Title: *Managing Anger*
Author: Gael Lindenfield
            ISBN: 0-00-710034-5

Title: *Preventing Face-to-Face Violence*
Author: Dr William Davies and Dr Neil Frued
            ISBN: 95209147-X

Title: *Essentials of Human Communication*
Author: Joseph DeVito
            ISBN: 0-673-99614-X
Title: *Psychology for A2 level*   **97**

Author: M Cardwell, L Clark & C Meldrum
              ISBN: 0-00-711512-1

Title: *Never be Lied to Again*
Author: David J. Lieberman
              ISBN: 0-312-20428-0

Title: *Managing Stress — Teach Yourself*
Author: T Looker & O Gregson
              ISBN: 0-340-66376-6

Title: *Think Safe, Act Safe, Stay Safe*
Author: Steve Collins
              ISBN: 0-00-710236-4

Title: *Words that Change Minds*
Author: Shelle Rose Charvet
              ISBN: 0-7872-3479-6

INDEX

ANY QUESTIONS?

If you have any questions, please feel free to email me at robert@verbal-aggression.com. Although I get a lot of email, I do try to answer it all.

Alternatively, get together with a group of friends or co-workers and form an action group to explore ways in which to deal with aggression in a peaceful and supportive way.

If you are interested in receiving a monthly newsletter via email that focuses on hints and tips to deal with Aggression, Violence and Stress Management, then visit my website at:

http://www.verbal-aggression.com

Also as my way of thanking you for reading this book, visit the website and you can download a free gift that will help you to deal with verbal aggression.